THE *Sisters* HAVE THEIR SAY

MORE INSIGHTS *from* GREAT WOMEN

WE ARE

THE FIRST GENERATION

OF BLACK PEOPLE

IN FOUR HUNDRED YEARS

who can live

our dreams.

—*Susan Taylor*

The Sisters Have Their Say

The quoted ideas expressed in this book (but not scripture verses) are not, in all cases, exact quotations, as some have been edited for clarity and brevity. In all cases, the author has attempted to maintain the speaker's original intent. In some cases, quoted material for this book was obtained from secondary sources, primarily print media. While every effort was made to ensure the accuracy of these sources, the accuracy cannot be guaranteed. For additions, deletions, corrections or clarifications in future editions of this text, please e-mail ContactUs@ElmHillBooks.com.

Cover Design and Page Layout: Margaret Pesek

Managing Editor: Alice Sullivan

ISBN 1-4041-8588-7 *(hardcover)*

ANTOINETTE HARGROVE

Originally from Huntsville, Alabama, Antoinette Hargrove is the 10th of 13 children. She received her Bachelor of Science degree in Business Administration from Athens State College and a Masters of Science in Organizational leadership from Cumberland University, Lebanon, Tennessee. She is involved with non-profit development, fundraising and volunteer coordination. In 2005, Ms. Hargrove became the proud foster mother of two young boys, John and Justin. She currently resides in Nashville, Tennessee and is very active in her local church where she seeks to minister to children and the elderly.

THE SISTERS HAVE THEIR SAY

Table of Contents

INTRODUCTION

—✺—

Many African-American women have received notable recognition for their extraordinary achievements. In this book, *The Sisters Have Their Say,* we celebrate the lives of women all over the world whose experiences serve as sources of inspiration.

Each narrative briefly shows the tenacity and the courage that these women had in various circumstances as they fought through barriers of racial discrimination or waged war against various types of abuse to accomplish their dreams and goals. Despite many obstacles, these strong women persevered.

Their voices have influenced a new generation. Their words and actions and dreams have challenged us to be better women by teaching us that our strength comes from the tiny voice that speaks to our heart and soul. Anything is possible. Every goal is attainable. Every person is valuable. Refuse to be a prisoner of the past. *When we stand up to speak, we make the world stand still and listen.*

Chapter 1
GROWING IN GRACE
PROF. WANGARI MAATHAI

—⚒—

I have always believed that solutions to most of our problems must come from us.

—*Prof. Wangari Maathai*

From the time Wangari Maathai was a child, her formative experiences and observations of nature in rural Kenya led to her dreams of improving the quality of life for women. It has been through her efforts of fighting for peace that women in her community and in other rural areas are now able to reap the rewards of a bountiful harvest.

Internationally recognized as the first woman from Africa to be awarded the Nobel Peace Prize for "her contribution to sustainable development, democracy and peace," she wears a badge of honor not awarded to many and takes her title seriously. Through the unique, down-to-earth concept of planting trees, now widely recognized as The Green Belt Movement, she stood at the forefront and assisted women in planting more than 20 million trees. The Green Belt Movement is an inspiring story for people working at the grassroots level to improve their environment.

It has been through this growing endeavor that she continues to fight for human rights and improving the quality of life for women. While her own road to success has not been easy, her voice has empowered others to change their situation.

Maathai herself has put it like this: "We are sharing our resources in a very inequitable way. We have parts of the world that are very deprived and parts of the world that are very rich. And that is partly the reason why we have conflicts." Maathai says the trees are a symbol for peace and conflict resolution. If the world is to grow in grace, mankind must raise their voice and give back to the world. She encourages others to provide hope for future generations by promoting peace and restoring natural resources. The choice is ours. Growth comes in numbers and peace comes with grace.

No one does it alone.

> —*Oprah Winfrey*

*This is a journey. Believe what you're doing
and why you're doing it.*

> —*Vanessa Davis Griggs*

*Every day that dawns is a reason to say,
"Thank You, Father."*

> —*Johnnetta Cole*

Surround yourself only with people who are going to lift you higher.

　　　　　　　—Oprah Winfrey

We make a living by what we get, but we make a life by what we give.

　　　　　　　—Barbara Harris

AFRICAN-AMERICAN FIRSTS

—⚬—

Sadie T. M. Alexander

First African-American female to receive

a Doctorate in Economics

The roots of happiness grow best in the soil of service.

—Ruth B. Love

We are positively a unique people.
Breathtaking people. Anything we do, we
do big! Despite attempts to stereotype us, we
are crazy, individual, and uncorralable people.

—Leontyne Price

AFRICAN-AMERICAN FIRSTS

—◊◊◊—

Susie Baker King Taylor

First African-American
Army Nurse

God is just. When he created man he made him in his image and never intended one should misuse the other. All men are born free and equal in his sight.

—Susie Baker King Taylor

The true worth of a race must be measured by the character of its womanhood.

—Mary McLeod Bethune

Chapter 2
LASTING FAITH
OPRAH WINFREY

—⁓—

Faith sustains me... Faith that, no matter what,
no matter how difficult life becomes, I'll be okay.

—*Oprah Winfrey*

Named *Orpah,* from the Book of Ruth in the Bible, the letters R and P were accidentally transposed and Oprah eventually became her accepted name. Born a black southerner out of wedlock and into abject poverty, Oprah has faced many kinds of hardships. However, these challenges have served as opportunities to launch her destiny both professionally and personally.

Faith and Focus helped her remove the grip of despair, when, as a troubled adolescent, she was sexually assaulted by a male relative. She fought frantically to beat the struggles of her youth and although many obstacles haunted Oprah, her voice ultimately became the voice for millions. She became an inspiration. Her power has influenced the world to change.

Oprah indeed confirmed that black women do not need to follow trends, we set them.

Through the power of the media, Oprah Winfrey has created an unparalleled connection with people around the world. She is unquestionably one of the wealthiest women in the United States, but her life story reveals the truth about the price tag that is sometimes attached to wealth.

Oprah said she survived because of her faith in a power that is greater than she. Faith is still the core of her life and she inspires others to use their abilities to make a difference in the lives of others.

*I figure if God believed in me so much that
He chose me, the least I can do is listen to what
He says and follow His every lead.*

—*Vanessa Davis Griggs*

To believe is to become what you believe.

—*June Jordan*

*It's pretty hard for the Lord to guide you if
you haven't made up your mind which way
you want to go.*

—*Madame C.J. Walker*

ALL OF US HAVE A GOD IN US,
AND THAT GOD IS THE SPIRIT
THAT UNITES ALL LIFE, EVERYTHING
THAT IS ON THIS PLANET. IT MUST
BE THIS VOICE THAT IS TELLING ME
TO DO SOMETHING, AND I AM SURE
IT'S THE SAME VOICE THAT IS
SPEAKING TO EVERYBODY ON THIS
PLANET—AT LEAST EVERYBODY
WHO SEEMS TO BE CONCERNED
ABOUT THE FATE OF THE WORLD,
THE FATE OF THIS PLANET.

—*Wangari Maathai*

*People see God every day; they just don't
recognize him.*

—Pearl Bailey

*If your faith can't move mountains, it should
at least climb them.*

—Queen Mother Moore

In the darkest moments I can still find peace.

—Marion Anderson

AFRICAN-AMERICAN FIRSTS

—⁓—

Jacquelyn Barrett

First African-American female sheriff,
Fulton County, Georgia

It's time to step out on faith, I've gotta show my faith. / It's been illusive for so long but freedom is mine today.

—India Arie

While I know myself as a creation of God, I am also obligated to realize and remember that everyone else and everything else are also God's creation.

—Maya Angelou

What God has intended for you goes far beyond anything you can imagine.

—Oprah Winfrey

African-American Firsts

—*m*—

Phyllis A. Wallace

First African-American female to receive

a Doctorate in Economics from Yale

I PRAY HARD,
WORK HARD, AND
LEAVE THE REST
TO GOD.

—Florence Griffith Joyner

Inspiration! Who can sing thy force? /
Or who describe the swiftness of thy course?

—Phyllis Wheatley

I have learned that the more we understand how very much God loves us, and the more we comprehend the grace He has demonstrated towards us, the more humble we become.

—Serita Ann Jakes

If you are obedient to God's word and are committed to fulfilling His plans for your life, you can face your fears with the assurance that God is in control of the situation.

—Thelma Wells

Chapter 3
LIFE CHALLENGES
HALLE BERRY

—⁓—

There'd never been another time in my life when I thought that I would not survive it. I've always been a survivor

—Halle Berry

All of her life, Halle Berry has been valued for her beauty. She was an adorable child who grew up with a mixed-race heritage in a family plagued by alcoholism and physical abuse. The struggles in her household were only the beginning of the cruelty she received since whites rejected her and blacks ridiculed her.

This beauty queen still struggles with racism and prejudice, and health-related issues such as diabetes, but she has found a way of escape by dazzling the world with her charisma and character. The first African-American female to win the Academy Award for best actress has shown the world more than beauty. Her talent and tenacious abilities allow her to enjoy a level of success that comes from years of hard work.

Her blooming popularity led to a multi-million dollar contract with Revlon, but no matter how the world perceives her, her beauty is just a reflection of the kind of beauty that develops from the true heart of a woman.

AFRICAN-AMERICAN FIRSTS

Halle Berry

*First African-American female to win
the Academy Award for Best Actress*

Being black has made me sensitive to any group who finds limitations put on it.

—Eleanor Holmes Norton

Treat failure as practice shots.

—Deborah McGriff

It is time for blacks to begin to shift from a war-time to a peace time identity from fighting for opportunity to the seizing of it.

—Shelby Steele

I DON'T BELIEVE
THAT LIFE IS SUPPOSED
TO MAKE YOU FEEL GOOD,
OR TO MAKE YOU FEEL
MISERABLE EITHER.
LIFE IS JUST SUPPOSED
TO MAKE YOU FEEL.

—Gloria Naylor

Poor people are allowed the same dreams as everyone else.

—Kimi Gray

The function of the family is to celebrate the triumphs and heroes of the black struggle and to remember the defeats.

—Janice Hall Benson

The dream is the truth.

—Zora Neale Hurston

Every man has a place in the world, but no man has the right to designate that place.

—*Pearl Bailey*

The purpose of evil was to survive it.

—*Toni Morrison*

The most rewarding freedom is freedom of the mind.

—*Amy Jacques Garvey*

CHALLENGES COME SO
WE CAN GROW AND BE
PREPARED FOR THINGS WE
ARE NOT EQUIPPED TO HANDLE
NOW. WHEN WE FACE
OUR CHALLENGES WITH FAITH,
PREPARED TO LEARN, WILLING
TO MAKE CHANGES, AND
IF NECESSARY, TO LET GO, WE
ARE DEMANDING OUR POWER
BE TURNED ON.

—*Iyanla Vanzant*

No child is ever spoiled by too much attention.
It is the lack of attention that spoils.

—*Bessie Blake*

Simply having children does not necessarily
make a woman a mother.

—*Mary Futrell*

God gives us permission to forget our past and
the understanding to live our present.

—*Serita Ann Jakes*

Chapter 4
SUCCESS
MAE C. JEMISON
—⚹—

There's no one route to success, but a big part of it involves believing in yourself, expecting it and preparing for it.

—*Mae C. Jemison*

The future never looked so bright for Dr. Mae Jemison, the first African-American woman to become an Astronaut and set foot in space. Blasting into orbit was just one of the many extraordinary successes for this pioneering woman.

As a young child, Jemison was afraid of heights. However, she made preparations to reach her dream of going into space and it was through her determination, energy and drive that she found success. Even though she loved to read and dance, her extensive background in science led to her dream of one day working for the National Aeronautics and Space Administration (NASA).

Her success is evident as she shows people that they can be anybody they want to be. Jemison holds many titles such as chemical engineer, scientist, physician, teacher and astronaut, and she is committed to improving the lives of others by teaching people in poor countries about medicine. She believes that a big part of success truly involves believing in oneself.

YOU LEARN SUCCESS
OR FAILURE FROM THE
ADULTS AROUND YOU.

—*Mae C. Jemison*

You can't just sit there and wait for people to give you that golden dream, you've got to get out there and make it happen for yourself.

—*Diana Ross*

I had to make my own living and my own opportunity... Don't sit down and wait for the opportunities to come; you have to get up and make them.

—*Madame C. J. Walker*

Our people are just waiting to read words written about them by their own authors.

—*Lana Turner*

The key to succeeding in a workplace where you are the only black person is to hold strong to your internal power.

—*Andrea D. Pinkney*

Whatever the white man has done, we have done, and done better.

—*Mary McLeod Bethune*

AFRICAN-AMERICAN FIRSTS

Mary Frances Berry

*First African-American female
to head a major research university,
University of Colorado*

*No matter what accomplishments you make,
somebody helps you.*

—Althea Gibson

*Of all the qualities necessary for success,
none comes before character.*

—Ernesta Procope

*To struggle and battle and overcome and
absolutely defeat every force designed against
us is the only way to achieve.*

—Nannie Helen Burroughs

GREATNESS IS DEFINED
BY SOMEONE WHO IS NOT SIMPLY
AWESOME AND WONDERFUL
IN THE SPORT THEY COMPETE
IN BUT GOES BEYOND THAT
AND IS GREAT IN WHATEVER THEY
DO OFF THE TRACK OR OFF
THE COURT. THEY CAN MAKE
A DIFFERENCE IN THE WORLD,
WHETHER IT'S BY HELPING KIDS
OR HELPING PEOPLE IN NEED.

—*Marion Jones*

In America, with education and hard work, it really does not matter where you came from; it matters only where you are going.

— *Condoleezza Rice*

If you are committed to pursuing your dreams, you must expect that you will run up against those who feel you can't do the job.

— *Mary Futrell*

I was a tough child. I was too large
and too poor to fit, and I fought back.

—Ethel Waters

I used to want the words
"She tried" on my tombstone.
Now I want "She did it."

—Katherine Dunham

Success doesn't come to you…you go to it.

—Marva Collins

*I learned that what you give comes back
to you. If we're members of society, we have
to support that society. These are things
I learned by example.*

—Mae C. Jemison

*Some of us aren't prepared to accept success—
especially someone else's.*

—Sarah Vaughan

Chapter 5
SACRIFICES
CORETTA SCOTT KING

—⁓—

When you are willing to make sacrifices for a great cause, you will never be alone.

—Coretta Scott King

The ability to make great sacrifices has been the strength of Coretta Scott King, widow of the late civil rights activist, Dr. Martin Luther King, Jr. Mrs. King was exposed early on to the injustices of life in a segregated society. This society in which she lived prevented her from being treated equally because of the color of her skin.

With her first love of music and the dreams of becoming an opera singer, she willingly sacrificed her plans and graciously accepted her role as a wife and a mother. This sacrifice would later change her life forever, as she became affectionately referred to as the "first lady" of the civil rights movement.

Choosing to walk side by side with her husband, her hope of racial equality inspired citizens, both black and white, to defy the segregation laws. This same hope would serve as a source of inspiration as she coped with the death of her husband in later years.

Channeling her grief, Mrs. King concentrated her energies on fulfilling her husband's work by keeping his dream alive. A noted community leader in her own right, she continues to speak out for human rights and freedom for all people.

*I will always be out here doing the things
I do, and I'm not going to stop talking
about Martin and promoting what I think
is important in terms of teaching other people,
particularly young people, his meaning so they
can live in such a way to make a contribution
to our advancement and progress.*

—*Coretta Scott King*

*The dream is real, my friends. The failure to
make it work is the unreality.*

—*Toni Cade Bambara*

Hate is too great a burden to bear. It injures the hater more than it injures the hated.

—Coretta Scott King

Don't feel entitled to anything you didn't sweat and struggle for.

—Marian Wright Edelman

Segregation was wrong when it was forced by white people, and I believe it is still wrong when it is requested by black people.

—Coretta Scott King

AFRICAN-AMERICAN FIRSTS

——◈——

Bessie Coleman

*First African-American
female Aviator*

*I really don't think life is about the
I-could-have-beens. Life is only about the
I-tried-to-do. I don't mind the failure but
I can't imagine that I'd forgive myself
if I didn't try.*

> —Nikki Giovanni

*The best way to live in this world is
to live above it.*

> —Sonia Sanchez

*As soon as healing takes place, go out
and heal somebody else.*

> —Maya Angelou

STRUGGLE IS
A NEVER ENDING PROCESS.
FREEDOM IS NEVER
REALLY WON. YOU EARN
IT AND WIN IT IN
EVERY GENERATION.

Coretta Scott King

Black America must never forget the price
paid for today's progress and promise.

—Johnnetta Cole

Women, if the soul of the nation is to be
saved, I believe that you must become its soul.

—Coretta Scott King

Everybody wants to do something to help,
but nobody wants to be first.

—Pearl Bailey

We have to help black men, but not at the expense of our own personalities as women.

　　　　　　　—Shirley Chisholm

It isn't where you came from, it's where you're going that counts.

　　　　　　　—Ella Fitzgerald

It is a burden of black people that we have to do more than talk.

　　　　　　　—Barbara Jordan

WHEN IT'S JUST US,
I CAN BE MYSELF
AND KNOW YOU'LL LOVE
AND UNDERSTAND ME
NO MATTER WHAT.
YOU DON'T WANT
ANYTHING FROM ME
EXCEPT MY HAPPINESS.

Coretta Scott King

Chapter 6
CHANGE
MAYA ANGELOU
—⚮—

If you don't like something, change it. If you can't change it, change your attitude. Don't complain.

—Maya Angelou

Maya Angelou, born Marguerite Annie Johnson, is considered one of the most prominent authors and poets and has long been one of the strongest voices for civil rights activism in America.

The voice that she now uses to speak against injustices with was once silent for nearly five years due to a violent sexual assault that left her without words. A black girl in a world whose boundaries were set by others, it wasn't until several years later that she realized how to use her words to invoke change.

She began to write, and it was her often disrupted life that inspired her to write her own life story, *I Know Why The Caged Bird Sings.*

Using the pride that was instilled in her at a very young age, Angelou exercised the pattern of suffering, of sacrifice and hope as a driving force for change. Several pivotal experiences served as turning points in her life and urged her to seek justice and answers through her personal expression of writing. She sensed the richness of black history and began to write for future generations. Through the freedom of writing, Angelou has become a voice of change.

Experience comes from falling, falling and smiling and picking yourself up and moving on.

—Mae C. Jemison

Why hate when you could spend your time doing other things?

—Miriam Makeba

Love is that condition in the human spirit so profound that it allows me to survive, and better than that, to thrive with passion, compassion, and style.

—Maya Angelou

Talk without effort is nothing.

　　　　　—Maria W. Stewart

*You really can change the world if you
care enough.*

　　　　　—Marian Wright Edelman

*There is a spirit and a need and a man
at the beginning of every great human
advance. Each of these must be right for
that particular moment of history, or
nothing happens.*

　　　　　—Coretta Scott King

AFRICAN-AMERICAN FIRSTS

—⁂—

CeCe Winans

*First African-American female
to win "female vocalist of the year"
Dove Award*

*My parents were always philosophizing
about how to bring about change. To me,
people who didn't try to make the world
a better place were strange.*

—Carol Moseley-Braun

*At fifteen, life had taught me
undeniably that surrender, in its place,
was as honorable as resistance, especially
if one had no choice.*

—Maya Angelou

*Instead of always looking at the past,
I put myself ahead twenty years and
try to look at what I need to do now
in order to get there then.*

—*Diana Ross*

*You've got to rattle your cage door.
You've got to let them know that you're
in there, and that you want out.*

—*Florence Kennedy*

—m—

Wangari Maathai

*First African woman
to be awarded the Nobel Prize in Peace;
first woman in central or eastern
Africa to hold a Ph.D.;
first woman head of a university
department in Kenya*

Do not call for black power or green power.
Call for brain power.

　　　　　　　　　—*Barbara Jordan*

Whenever there is chaos, it creates wonderful
thinking. Chaos is a gift.

　　　　　　　　　—*Septima Clark*

I have never been constrained except that
I made the prison.

　　　　　　　　　—*Mari Evans*

If you always do what you always did,
you will always get what you always got.

—Moms Mabley

If you can't teach me, don't criticize me.

—Sonya Carson

Chapter 7
SPIRITUAL BALANCE
CeCe Winans

—∿—

The church was an important stabilizer in my life as a young person.

—CeCe Winans

The entertainment industry has given us CeCe Winans, but to her family and friends she is Pricilla Love. The first Black woman to win the coveted "female vocalist of the year" Dove Award, CeCe has a unique sound which is a mixture of gospel, R&B and jazz. Her style of music has touched people's lives in many ways. The eighth of ten children, CeCe says she "just loves good music, music with a positive message."

Humbly accepting the multiple roles as a world-renowned singer, a caring daughter and sister, and a loving mother and wife, she boldly maintains the spiritual balance that kept her grounded. She says, "The church was an important stabilizer in my life as a young person. It was important to find a place where my children could feel that same thing."

Her spiritual passion also allows her to use her songs as ministry. In her book, *On a Positive Note,* CeCe Winans talks about her faith, her life in music, and her everyday blessings. Like many working mothers, CeCe has changed the rules and allowed her spiritual stability to balance her family and career. She puts on the best performance of her life by humbly demonstrating to each of us the strength and determination that's needed to balance multiple roles.

I THINK IF WE'RE GOING
TO RECLAIM OR RECAPTURE
YOUNG PEOPLE,
IT'S GOING TO HAVE
TO BE THROUGH THE CHURCH
OR SPIRITUALITY.

—*Bernice King*

*I have prayed my way out of so many
situations. When I say that, I mean that my
faith is strengthened by praying. I repeat the very
Word of God—scripture verses—in my prayers.
This reminds me of God's promises never to
leave or forsake me, to heal, and to restore.*

—*Tiffany L. Warren*

*I need my church in order to keep going. Church
is my favorite place to be. When I am in the
Lord's presence surrounded by brothers and
sisters I feel love and strength. We go to church
expecting to be changed. It's a life-giving place.*

—*CeCe Winans*

YOU MUST BE WILLING
TO GIVE TOTAL
UNCONDITIONAL LOVE
TO EVERYONE,
UNDER ALL CIRCUMSTANCES.
THAT MEANS BEING
WILLING TO BE TOTALLY
RESPONSIBLE FOR WHAT YOU
DO AND HOW YOU DO IT.

—*Iyanla Vanzant*

Please pray for those who are too consumed with themselves or other people's problems to see God at work in their lives.

—Thelma Wells

There is no secret that can separate you from God's love; there is no secret that can separate you from His blessings; there is no secret that is worth keeping from His grace.

—Serita Ann Jakes

Trust is to human relationships what faith is to gospel living. It is the beginning place, the foundation upon which more can be built. Where trust is, love can flourish.

—Barbara Smith

African-American Firsts

Joycelyn Elders

First African-American
U.S. Surgeon General

God's laws last longer than those who
break them.

—*Charlotte E. Ray*

Having God for my friend and portion,
what have I to fear? As long as it is the
will of God, I rejoice that I am as I am.

—*Maria W. Stewart*

Don't settle for average. Bring your best to
the moment. Then, whether it fails or
succeeds, at least you know you gave all you
had. We need to live the best that's in us.

—*Angela Bassett*

Chapter 8
PURPOSE
MAXINE WATERS

—⁓—

If you believe in something, you must be prepared to fight. To argue. To persuade.

—*Maxine Waters*

Maxine Waters was born in St. Louis, Missouri, as the fifth of 13 children reared by a single mother. She began working at age 13 in factories, segregated restaurants, and later, at a telephone company. After earning her college degree from California State University at Los Angeles, she began her career in public service as a teacher and as a volunteer coordinator in the Head Start program, a private nonprofit membership organization dedicated exclusively to providing comprehensive education, health, nutrition, and parent involvement services to low-income children and their families.

Now, after more than 25 years of public service, her outspoken voice has gained her a fearless reputation as an advocate for women, children, people of color and poor people. As an advocate for human rights and family reunification, Waters often tackles difficult and often controversial issues.

She is a co-founder of Black Women's Forum, a nonprofit organization of over 1,200 African-American women in the Los Angeles area. She is considered by many to be one of the most powerful women in American politics today. This courageous woman knows her purpose and she uses her talents and her visibility to support her passion.

An education…about ourselves would empower black women because it would help us understand the source of our powerlessness. And, understanding is always the first step towards change.

—Mary McLeod Bethune

We defeat oppression with liberty. We cure indifference with compassion. We remedy social injustice with justice. And if our journey embodies these lasting principles, we find peace.

—Patricia Roberts Harris

Liberation means you don't have to be silenced.

—Toni Morrison

AFRICAN-AMERICAN FIRSTS

—⁂—

Barbara Harris

*First African-American female
Protestant Episcopal Bishop*

My mission is to leave behind me the kind of impression that will make it easier for those who follow.

—Marian Anderson

Honey, it's so easy to talk a good game. What we need are folks who will do something!

—Maxine Waters

Living in the inner city is the same as living in the suburbs or surviving in the world. You have to know who you are, set goals in life, and maintain a self-image.

—Marva Collins

I've been in this struggle for many years now.
I understand racism. I understand that there are a
lot of people in this country who don't care about
the problems of the inner city. We have to fight
every day that we get up for every little thing that
we get. And so I keep struggling.

—Maxine Waters

Don't be upset if your dreams don't come true.
It could be the best thing that ever happened
to you.

—Shari Belafonte

The kind of ancestors we have is not as important
as the kind of descendents our ancestors have.

—Phyllis A. Wallace

Our aim should be service, not success.

—*Barbara Smith*

The first sign of an educated person is that she asks more questions than she delivers answers.

—*Johnnetta Cole*

It is not so much what we know as how well we use what we know.

—*Ernesta Procope*

THIS NATION HAS
ALWAYS STRUGGLED WITH
HOW IT WAS GOING TO
DEAL WITH POOR PEOPLE
AND PEOPLE OF COLOR.

— *Maxine Waters*

Chapter 9
COURAGE
CAPTAIN CHRISTINA HOPPER

—⚔—

My faith gives me the consistent ability to cope with all kinds of stressors.

—Captain Christina Hopper

As one of only two female African-American pilots in the Air Force that she knows of, Captain Christina Hopper is a rarity. It takes tremendous faith to fight for what one believes in, but for this brave solider, her faith never faded. "I just trusted that if God wanted me to do this, he would give me the ability and the skill to go and do it," she said. And even with one of her greatest anxieties of being captured, she never dwelled on it.

Captain Hopper flew over 50 combat and combat support missions during her deployment in Iraq. Hopper faced treacherous conditions time and time again but she knew she could not turn back. Through the hostile combat and even though her fighter plane was struck by lightning once, she completed her missions.

She recalls, "The desert experience was unforgettable," but she said she looks back on that experience with a deep sense of gratitude. "I'm grateful to God, who gave the opportunity to take part in such a life-changing and world-changing event."

For her bravery in battle, Captain Hopper earned an Air Medal, one of the military's highest honors. And for her tour of duty in Iraq, she has been rewarded with a place in history—as the first African-American woman ever to fly a fighter jet in a combat mission of a major war.

A devout Christian, she says her faith kept her strong and gave her the courage to do what needed to be done: "I trusted that God would protect me." Her battlefield experience impacts each of us as she encourages us to see faith as not just a part of life, but rather as a central point.

We wanted something for ourselves and for our children, so we took a chance with our lives.

—Unita Blackwell

Lord, make me so uncomfortable that I will do the very thing I fear.

—Ruby Dee

If now isn't a good time for the truth, I don't see when we'll get to it.

—Nikki Giovanni

Truth-tellers are not always palatable.
There is a preference for candy bars.

       —Gwendolyn Brooks

I won't allow that word [guilt] in my life,
and I've forgotten how to spell it.

       —Diahann Carroll

No person is your friend who demands
your silence, or denies your right to grow.

       —Alice Walker

African-American Firsts

Patricia Roberts Harris

*First African-American female
in presidential cabinet, Secretary of Health,
Education and Welfare*

You have only one chance to make a first impression. Make it count.

—Markita Andrews

It's no disgrace to start over or to begin anew.

—Bebe Moore Campbell

To live is to suffer; to survive is to find some meaning in the suffering.

—Roberta Flack

DISABILITIES CAN
SOMETIMES BE DEFINITIONS.
YOU CAN THINK
OF YOURSELF IN TERMS OF
WHAT YOU CAN'T DO
AND NEVER REALIZE THE
POSSIBILITIES OF WHAT
YOU CAN DO.

—Bonnie St. John

AFRICAN-AMERICAN FIRSTS

Rita Dove

First African-American
U.S. Poet Laureate

Positive anything is better than negative nothing.

—Lorraine Hansberry

Fear is not a wall but an emotion. And like all emotions, it can be overcome.

—Gwen Goldsby Grant

Who can be born black and not exalt!

—Mari Evans

My message is about changing our way of thinking about women and abuses of power.

—Anita Hill

The prejudiced people can't insult you because they're blinded by their own ignorance.

—Pearl Bailey

The best way to fight poverty is with a weapon loaded with ambition.

—Septima Clark

Chapter 10
NEVER GIVE UP
MARION JONES

—⚏—

Losing puts things in perspective. If you win all the time, it would be easy to believe nobody could ever beat you. Losing reminds me there's going to be somebody out there who's going to pop onto the scene one day; just like I did and start winning.

—Marion Jones

Marion Jones sprinted into history by becoming the first woman to win five track medals in one Olympics: three gold, and two bronze. She is the first woman since Florence Griffith Joyner in 1988 to win three gold medals in track at an Olympics game.

Jones (born October 12, 1975 in Los Angeles, California) holds dual citizenship from the USA and Belize. Jones discovered her gift for speed as a kid, chasing her brothers around the neighborhood when she was just five. The fastest woman, and arguably the best female athlete in the world, Marion can outrun just about anyone on the track. But she wasn't able to escape the heartbreak and anger that marred her childhood.

Her father, George Jones, left the family when she was only two years old, and although Marion pursued her absentee father for years, he showed no interest in forming a bond with his daughter. Jones' mother remarried when Marion was five, finally giving her a father figure. But tragedy struck seven years later when her step-father died of a stroke.

Jones vented her grief and anger on the track. The hurdles she faced in life couldn't stop this all-purpose performer from following her dream. Watching women such as the great Flo Jo run, Marion was awestruck and made a promise to herself: she, too, would win Olympic Gold—and she did. It was Marion's determination and dedicated spirit that earned her the title of the world's best female sprinter.

Marion has become a role-model, not only for her athleticism, but also for her inspirational attitude and charismatic personality. Bright, beautiful and endlessly talented, she encourages other women to go all out in pursuit of their dreams.

*You don't make progress by standing on
the sidelines, whimpering and complaining.
You make progress by implementing ideas.*

—Shirley Chisholm

*Many people know how to criticize, but
few know how to praise.*

—Ethel Waters

We will band together and survive or live apart and die as fools.

—Susan Taylor

Failure is another stepping stone to greatness.

—Oprah Winfrey

Don't sit down and wait for the opportunities to come…Get up and make them!

—Madame C.J. Walker

WE CANNOT SILENCE
THE VOICES THAT
WE DO NOT LIKE HEARING.
WE CAN, HOWEVER,
DO EVERYTHING IN OUR
POWER TO MAKE CERTAIN
OTHER VOICES ARE HEARD.

—Deborah Prophrow-Stith M.D.

AFRICAN-AMERICAN FIRSTS

CAPTAIN CHRISTINA HOPPER

*First African-American female
to fly a fighter jet in a combat mission
of a major war*

Character is what you have left when you've lost everything else.

—Patricia Roberts Harris

As long as you keep a person down, some part of you has to be down there to hold him down, so it means you cannot soar as you otherwise might.

—Marian Anderson

I always had something to shoot for each year; to jump one inch farther.

—Jackie Joyner-Kersee

*Failure to recognize possibilities is the most
dangerous and common mistake one can make.*

—Mae Jemison

*Dream the biggest dream for yourself. Hold the
highest vision of life for yourself.*

—Oprah Winfrey

*This is our moment. I honestly wouldn't be
anyone but a black woman in America right now.
I feel that this is our time to break new ground.*

—Halle Berry

I refused to be discouraged, for neither God nor man could use a discouraged soul.

      —Mary McLeod Bethune

My mother made me strong. Watching her struggle to raise us and feed us made me want to be a stronger woman.

      —Mary J. Blige

It doesn't matter what you are trying to accomplish. It's all a matter of discipline.

—*Wilma Rudolph*

People may doubt what you say, but they will always believe what you do.

—*Nannie Helen Burroughs*

Chapter 11
TREASURES OF LIFE
DENYCE GRAVES

—⁓—

Real poverty is the loss of imagination.

—Denyce Graves

Particularly well known to operatic audiences, Denyce Graves combines her expressive vocalism and exceptional gifts for communication with her dynamic stage presence, enriching audiences around the world. Her voice has the power to move the human soul and can leave hearts filled with beautiful words and images beyond imagination.

Growing up in a rough neighborhood in Washington, D.C., her surroundings constantly insisted that her life had no value. Not willing to give up her hopes and ignore her gift, she used her voice and prevented her circumstances to limit her abilities. Even through several personal life struggles, including a failed marriage, depression, weight loss, and a delicate surgery on her vocal chords, she has maintained her charisma and her ability to captivate audiences.

As the appointed Cultural Ambassador for the United States, Graves now travels around the world appearing in good-will missions of musical performances, lectures, and seminars. The mezzo soprano diva has utilized her greatest treasure—her voice—and has touched many lives with her theatrical abilities that allow her to delight audiences all over the world.

I HOPE YOU WILL FIND
THAT BEING CREATIVE
WILL HELP YOU
IN ALL THAT YOU DO—
NO MATTER WHAT CAREER
PATH YOU CHOOSE.

—Denyce Graves

And so our mothers and grandmothers have, more often than not anonymously, handed on the creative sparks, the seed of the flower they themselves never hoped to see.

— *Alice Walker*

The only thing that can free you is the belief that you can be free.

— *Oprah Winfrey*

There is more pleasure in loving than in being loved.

— *Jeanne Moutoussamy-Ashe*

African-American Firsts

—⁓—

Dr. Mae Jemison

*First African-American
female Astronaut*

SOMETIMES YOU'VE GOT
TO LET EVERYTHING GO,
PURGE YOURSELF. I DID THAT,
I HAD NOTHING, BUT I HAD
MY FREEDOM...WHATEVER IS
BRINGING YOU DOWN, GET RID
OF IT. BECAUSE YOU'LL
FIND THAT WHEN YOU'RE FREE,
YOUR TRUE CREATIVITY,
YOUR TRUE SELF COMES OUT.

—Tina Turner

*We usually see things not as they are
but as we are.*

— *Louise Beavers*

*The most lonely place in the world is the
human heart when love is absent.*

— *Sadie T.M. Alexander*

*Love is like a virus. It can happen to
anybody at any time.*

— *Maya Angelou*

TEACH YOUR CHILDREN
THE INTERNALS AND THE
EXTERNALS, RATHER THAN
JUST THE EXTERNALS OF
CLOTHING AND MONEY.

—Nannie Burroughs

AFRICAN-AMERICAN FIRSTS

Vanessa Williams

First African-American
"Miss America"

*Love stretches your heart and makes you
big inside.*

　　　　　　　—*Margaret Walker*

Lifting as we climb.

—*Motto, National Association of Colored Women*

*Education is the jewel casting brilliance
into the future.*

　　　　　　　　—*Mari Evans*

THIS IS ONE OF
THE GLORIES OF MAN,
THE INVENTIVENESS OF THE
HUMAN MIND AND THE
HUMAN SPIRIT: WHENEVER
LIFE DOESN'T SEEM
TO GIVE AN ANSWER,
WE CREATE ONE.

— *Lorraine Hansberry*

Chapter 12
THE POWER WITHIN
IYANLA VANZANT

—⁓—

My greatest desire is for people to know who they are from the inside out and to use that knowledge as a tool of empowerment and love.

—*Iyanla Vanzant*

Iyanla (pronounced Ee-Youn La) Vanzant was born in 1953 in Brooklyn, N.Y. in the back seat of a taxicab and given the name Rhonda Fleming. Today we know her as a best-selling author, lawyer, and nationally recognized inspirational speaker. Of her work she says, it "teaches people how to move beyond whatever has happened in their lives in order to do and be what we came to life to do and be." Vanzant speaks from experience. Retained in the memory of this former welfare mother are numerous accounts of childhood abuse, rape and later spousal abuse. However, her ability to inspire others comes from the inherent power within her own story.

Her life path took her through multiple life-changing experiences that shaped her beliefs, the same beliefs that now empower women of all classes. She encourages women through profound insights to tap into the "power within" to take control of situations that trap them spiritually. Her work has become a source of great power as she gives confidence to people searching for happiness and spiritual growth. In her book, *One Day My Soul Just Opened Up,* Vanzant takes you on a 40-day spiritual journey to help you find yourself.

Iyanla (meaning "great mother" in Yoruba or Nigerian) conducts workshops and lectures to thousands around the country, hoping to inspire each listener to take a stand and create a better life, a better community, and a better world. Vanzant has received numerous awards and accolades for her work. She is a spiritual counselor with a message. There are no boundaries to helping oneself—the power is truly within each of us.

Tremendous amounts of talent are being lost to our society just because that talent wears a skirt.

—Shirley Chisholm

We must conquer our own doubts and fears. It is the greatest mistake to sit and do nothing. Each of us must do what we can.

—Jane Browning Smith

The best lessons, the best sermons are those that are lived.

—Yolanda King

If American women would increase their voting turnout by 10 percent, I think we would see an end to all of the budget cuts in programs benefiting women and children.

—Coretta Scott King

If you understand a person's origins, you can understand her. I've always had to take care of myself. I couldn't just be that sweet little girl who kept her mouth shut. Had I done that, I'd be long gone by now.

—Anita Baker

It is important for women, and especially African-American women, to become involved and to hold public office.

—Constance Baker Motley

My soul is full of concern and love, and I understand the meaning of my own life and the lives of others.

—Betty Shabazz

You have a right to your thoughts and feelings. Your feelings are always valid.

—Iyanla Vanzant

AFRICAN-AMERICAN FIRSTS

Marion Jones

*First woman to win five track medals
in one Olympics game*

I WASN'T CONCERNED
ABOUT THE HARDSHIPS
BECAUSE I ALWAYS FELT
I WAS DOING WHAT I HAD
TO DO, WHAT I WANTED
TO DO, AND WHAT I WAS
DESTINED TO DO.

—*Katherine Dunham*

Nothing is going to be handed to you. You have to make things happen.

—Florence Griffith Joyner

We must change in order to survive.

—Pearl Bailey

Your world is as big as you make it.

—Georgia Douglas Johnson

*Greatness is not measured by what
a man or woman accomplishes, but the
opposition he or she has to overcome to
reach his or her goals.*

—Dorothy Height

*We have been raised to fear the yes
in ourselves.*

—Audré Lorde

AMERICA BE PLACED
ON NOTICE. WE KNOW WHO
WE ARE. WE UNDERSTAND
OUR COLLECTIVE POWER.
FOLLOWING TODAY WE WILL
ACT ON THAT POWER.

—*Maxine Waters*

(Million Woman March 1997)

Chapter 13
KNOCKED DOWN, NOT OUT
VANESSA WILLIAMS

—∿—

*I hope my legacy will be that I was a survivor...
a woman who was her own person and persevered
time and time again.*

—*Vanessa Williams*

Vanessa Lynn Williams was born On March 18, 1963. The birth announcement read "Here she is, Miss America," and ironically 20 years later on September 17, 1983, she became the first African-American woman to be crowned "Miss America."

During her reign as Miss America, she was forced to resign her crown and many thought her future in show business was over. However, though knocked down, Williams was not out for the count. She said, "once you hit rock bottom the only place to go is up." Proving to herself and to Hollywood that her career was not through, she made one of the most amazing and unanticipated reappearances in show business history and turned her trials into triumphs.

Williams' struggle shows us the liberty that each of us have to choose to get up when we have fallen down. Her story encourages us to hear the internal voice that refuses to respond to excuses that tell us we aren't good enough, we aren't smart enough, or the struggle is just too hard. We can choose to be brave and dust off the pains of the past and move forward to a new beginning as we accept our own crown of glory.

THERE WILL ALWAYS
BE SOME CURVE BALLS
IN YOUR LIFE. TEACH YOUR
CHILDREN TO THRIVE
IN THAT ADVERSITY.

—Jeanne Moutoussamy-Ashe

The encountering [of defeats] may be the very experience which creates the vitality and the power to endure.

—Maya Angelou

Don't let anything stop you. There will be times when you'll be disappointed, but you can't stop.

—Sadie T.M. Alexander

Take a day to heal from the lies you've told yourself and the ones that have been told to you.

—Maya Angelou

One isn't necessarily born with courage, but one is born with potential. Without courage, we cannot practice any other virtue with consistency.

—Maya Angelou

Ours is the truest dignity of man, the dignity of the undefeated.

—Ethel Waters

Deal with yourself as an individual worthy of respect and make everyone else deal with you the same way.

—Nikki Giovanni

African-American Firsts

Florence Griffith Joyner

First woman to win three gold medals
in track at an Olympics game

Self-hate is a form of mental slavery
that results in poverty, ignorance and crime.

—*Susan Taylor*

Someone was hurt before you; wronged
before you; hungry before you; beaten before
you; humiliated before you; raped before you;
yet, someone survived.

—*Maya Angelou*

The first and worst of all frauds is to cheat one's self.

—*Pearl Bailey*

Love yourself, appreciate yourself,
see the good in you, see the God in you,
and respect yourself.

—*Betty Shabazz*

You asked me if I ever stood up for anything.
Yeah, I stood up for my life.

—*Tina Turner*

Chapter 14
DISCOVERING YOUR IDENTITY
ANTOINETTE HARGROVE

—∞—

The first step to being someone is being yourself.

—Antoinette Hargrove

I was born as the tenth of thirteen children. With seven older sisters, I wrestled for many years searching for my own identity. I struggled with a number of issues that often times made me ask the question, "What is my purpose in life?" As a result, my feelings of inadequacy prevented me from having peace. Being the youngest girl, I secretly wanted the life of my older siblings and time and time again, I daydreamed about the day when I would finally be a grown person, on my own.

But when I entered the real world, I began to really struggle with the consequences of some of the choices I had made. In my own search for love, I exposed myself to a pretender, a dreamer, and a drug user. It did not take long before I wanted to rush back to the comfort of our crowded home instead of being trapped in the body of a person who felt all alone. I desperately wanted a way of escape. I was living someone else's life, it was not my own. I knew this was not the direction that would fulfill my purpose. I began waging war against the youngest sister mentality that often made me want to lean on my older sisters. I resisted and refused to allow my obsession with my family to define me, I had to find and define myself.

Years later, I was the keynote speaker at a church and gave an inspirational message, "A Case of Mistaken Identity." Although I wrote the message to inspire others, I realized that the loneliness I felt as a child was because I had not focused on my relationship with Christ. I became convicted by my own words. The first step to being someone is being yourself. Christ knew His purpose, why shouldn't I? I was determined to discover myself and reach my goals. Now I am confident that in my role as a foster mother, I have an internal peace which is the perfect gift, given to me from above.

Today, I leave this message for women all over the world. We must stop neglecting one of the most fundamental rules of life—simply know yourself. This journey of life will end someday, but the true beginning of life is when you become acquainted with the spirit of the person inside.

YOU CANNOT
BELONG TO ANYONE
ELSE UNTIL YOU
BELONG TO YOURSELF.

—Pearl Bailey

You better appreciate what you have before you haven't.

—*CeCe Winans*

I've made mistakes; we all do. But I don't believe that you have to have done it before to do it well. You only have to be smart and talented to do it well.

—*Suzanne De Passe*

I have learned that I am nothing but I have the power to have everything.

—*Antoinette Hargrove*

African-American Firsts

—⁓—

Charlotte E. Ray

First African-American
female lawyer

It's when we forget ourselves that we accomplish tasks that are most likely to be remembered.

　　　　　　—Bessie Coleman

Even the longest journey begins with a single step.

　　　　　　—Author Unknown

See what you see is what you get, / and oh, you ain't seen nothing yet.

　　　　　　—Lauryn Hill

Never be afraid to sit awhile and think.

—Lorraine Hansberry

*The most important thing is to just
enjoy yourself.*

—Marion Jones

*Brown skin, you know I love your
brown skin. / I can't tell where yours
begins, I can't tell where mine ends.*

—India Arie

CHARACTER IS WHAT
YOU KNOW YOU ARE,
NOT WHAT OTHERS
THINK YOU HAVE.

—*Marva Collins*

There is no path. The path is made by walking.

—Author Unknown

I never intended to be a run-of-the-mill person.

—Barbara Jordan

*When I was a child, it did not occur
to me, even once, that the black in which
I was encased (I called it brown in those days)
would be considered, one day, beautiful.*

—Gwendolyn Brooks

JUST DON'T GIVE UP
TRYING TO DO WHAT YOU
REALLY WANT TO DO.
WHERE THERE'S LOVE AND
INSPIRATION, I DON'T THINK
YOU CAN GO WRONG.

—Ella Fitzgerald

Chapter 15
WOMEN LIKE US

—⁂—

In my world, black women can do anything.

—Julie Dash

Black women know what we are looking for. We have removed roadblocks on the way to our destinations, we have refused to accept the message from society that tells us who we should or should not be. We are here, we are alive, and as sisters, we must have our say.

We are on the move, on the rise. We are pressing on and changing the way that society regards all women. The struggles of the African-American woman have not been without hardships, but with a tremendous amount of faith, determination, and courage, we have overcome.

We are powerful women in positions to influence people with our voices, our thoughts, and our examples. We are uplifting the black community to improve the quality of life for all people. Our strength is reflected in the faces of women of the 21st century. Women like us are listening as the sisters have their say.

The legacy of courage left by heroic black women was amassed, deed by deed, day by day, without praise or encouragement.

— *Johnetta Cole*

We as black women must understand the true power all of us bring to each other and to the struggle.

— *Belynda B. Bady*

Our ancestors are an ever-widening circle of hope.

—*Toni Morrison*

An artist represents an oppressed people and makes revolution irresistible.

—*Toni Cade Bambara*

Black women as a group have never been fools. We couldn't afford to be.

—*Barbara Smith*

AFRICAN-AMERICAN FIRSTS

—w—

Condoleezza Rice

First African-American
National Security Advisor

I feel good every day I open my eyes because I have a good soul. I feel good about who I am, what I am, where I'm from, and where I'm going. But above all, I love myself.

—Terry B. Williams

Look at me. I am black. I am beautiful.

—Mary McLeod Bethune

You must understand, being black…means being committed to furthering our race and nurturing our children.

—Elizabeth Ridley

I HAVE SEEN THAT THE
WORLD IS TO THE STRONG,
REGARDLESS OF
A LITTLE PIGMENTATION
MORE OR LESS.

—*Zora Neale Hurston*

*You are my sister, and what you do will have
an impact on me and every other sister. If
you hurt, I hurt. When you rejoice, I rejoice.*

—*Terry B. Williams*

*You don't get there because, you get there
in spite of.*

—*Janet Colins*

*We have a right to a diversity of voices.
We are diverse. We don't have to all agree
on everything.*

—*Jill Nelson*

YOU HAVE TO BE ABLE—
BE WILLING—TO TEACH
YOUR SON, JUST AS
YOU WOULD TEACH YOUR
DAUGHTER, WHAT IT IS
TO RESPECT ANOTHER
HUMAN BEING.

—Andrea Thompson Adam

Your ancestors took the lash, the branding iron, humiliations, and oppression, because one day they believed you would come along to flesh out the dream.

—*Maya Angelou*

Family faces are…mirrors. Looking at people who belong to us, we see the past, present, and future.

—*Gail Lumet Buckley*

We need leadership that thinks about the future and asks us to invest ourselves.

—*Anita DeFrantz*

The motto I taught my boys was "Aim at the Sun!" If you do not bring it down, you will shoot higher than if you had aimed at the earth.

—Rebecca Steward

You don't have to be born with a silver spoon in your mouth to end up at the end of the golden rainbow.

—Dianne Wilkerson

Individual ideas, like breaths, are waiting to be drawn from unlimited supply.

—Margaret Danner

Sources

Andrea Thompson Adam	Los Angeles Commission on Assaults Against Women official
Sadie T.M. Alexander	Lawyer and Activist
Marion Anderson	Opera Star
Markita Andrews	Girl Scout who holds record for cookie sales
Maya Angelou	Novelist and Poet
India Arie	R&B Singer
Belynda B. Bady	Entrepreneur
Pearl Bailey	Entertainer
Anita Baker	Singer
Toni Cade Bambara	Writer
Jacquelyn Barret	Sheriff
Angela Bassett	Actress
Louise Beavers	Silent-Film Star
Shari Belafonte	Actress
Janice Hall Benson	Psychologist
Halle Berry	Actress

Sources

Mary McLeod Bethune	Educator
Unita Blackwell	Civil Rights Activist
Bessie Blake	Mother
Mary J. Blige	R&B Singer
Gwendolyn Brooks	Poet and Writer
Gail Lumet Buckley	Writer
Nannie Helen Burroughs	Educator and Civil Rights Activist
Bebe Moore Campbell	Journalist and Writer
Diahann Carroll	Singer
Sonya Carson	Former Teenage Mother
Shirley Chisholm	Politician
Septima Clark	Educator and Civil Rights Activist
Janet Colins	Prima Ballerina
Marva Collins	Educator
Johnnetta Cole	President of Spelman College
Bessie Coleman	Pilot

Sources
—∞—

Margaret Danner	Poet
Julie Dash	Filmmaker
Anita DeFrantz	Lawyer and Athlete
Suzanne De Passe	President, Gordy/De Passe Productions
Ruby Dee	Actress
Katherine Dunham	Dancer, Choreographer, Advisor to the cultural ministry of Senegal
Marian Wright Edelman	Children's Defense Fund Official
Mari Evans	Poet
Ella Fitzgerald	Singer
Roberta Flack	Singer
Mary Futrell	Educator
Amy Jacques Garvey	Nationalist leader
Althea Gibson	Tennis Champion
Nikki Giovanni	Poet, Lecturer and Essayist
Gwen Goldsby Grant	Psychologist

Sources

Denyce Graves   Opera Singer

Kimi Gray   Late President of the Kenilworth-Parkside Resident Management Corporations

Vanessa Davis Griggs   Writer and Speaker

Lorraine Hansberry   Playwright and Activist

Antoinette Hargrove   Lecturer, Educator, and Activist

Barbara Harris   Protestant Episcopal Bishop

Patricia Roberts Harris   Former U.S. Secretary of Health, Education and Welfare

Dorothy Height   National Council of Negro Women official

Anita Hill   Law Professor

Lauryn Hill   R&B Singer

Captain Christina Hopper   Fighter Pilot

Zora Neale Hurston   Writer and Folklorist

Serita Ann Jakes   Writer and Speaker

Sources

Mae C. Jemison — Doctor, Engineer, and Astronaut

Georgia Douglas Johnson — Writer

Marion Jones — Olympic Track Star

Barbara Jordan — Lawyer and U.S. Congresswoman

June Jordan — Poet and Essayist

Florence Griffith Joyner — Olympic Track star

Florence Kennedy — Lawyer and Feminist

Jackie Joyner-Kersee — Athlete and Olympic Gold Medalist

Bernice King — Minister

Coretta Scott King — Activist

Yolanda King — Actress and Activist

Audré Lorde — Writer

Ruth B. Love — Educator

Wangari Maathai — Nobel Peace Prize Winner, Activist, and Educator

Moms Mabley (Jackie Mabley) — Comedian

Sources

Miriam Makeba | Folksinger

Deborah McGriff | Educator

Queen Mother Moore | Activist

Toni Morrison | Writer

Carol Moseley-Braun | U.S. Senator

Constance Baker Motley | Lawyer and Judge

Jeanne Moutoussamy-Ashe | Photographer

Gloria Naylor | Writer

Jill Nelson | Writer

Eleanor Holmes Norton | Lawyer and Activist

Andrea D. Pinkney | Writer

Deborah Prophrow-Stith M.D. | Dean of Harvard Schoo of Public Health

Leontyne Price | Opera Singer

Ernesta Procope | CEO, E.G. Bowman Company

Charlotte E. Ray | Lawyer

Condoleezza Rice | U.S. National Security Advisor

Elizabeth Ridley | Educator

Sources

—※—

Diana Ross	Singer
Wilma Rudolph	Olympic Gold Medalist
Sonia Sanchez	Poet
Betty Shabazz	Activist
Barbara Smith	Former Model and Restaurateur
Jane Browning Smith	Director, Inroads, Inc.
Bonnie St. John	Athlete and Scholar
Shelby Steele	Writer and Editor
Rebecca Steward	Mother
Maria W. Stewart	Lecturer
Susan Taylor	Editor and Writer
Susie Baker King Taylor	Army Nurse
Sojourner Truth	Abolitionist and Women's Rights Advocate
Lana Turner	Book club founder
Tina Turner	Singer
Iyanla Vanzant	Author, Lawyer, and Speaker

Sources

—m—

Sarah Vaughan	Jazz Legend
Alice Walker	Prize-Winning Author and Activist
Madame C.J. Walker	Entrepreneur and Activist
Margaret Walker	Writer
Phyllis A. Wallace	Economist
Ethel Waters	Singer, Dancer, and Actress
Maxine Waters	Politician
Thelma Wells	Writer and Women of Faith Speaker
Phyllis Wheatley	Poet
Dianne Wilkerson	Politician
Terry B. Williams	Civilian Employee of the New York Police Department (NYPD)
Vanessa Williams	Former "Miss America" and Spokeswoman
CeCe Winans	Gospel Singer
Oprah Winfrey	Entertainer and Entrepreneur